Bound

Also by Jubi Arriola-Headley

Original Kink

Bound

Poems **Jubi Arriola-Headley**

A Karen & Michael Braziller Book

PERSEA BOOKS / NEW YORK

Persea Books, Inc.
90 Broad Street
New York, New York 10004

LIBRARY OF CONGRESS CATALOGING-IN-PUBLICATION DATA

Names: Arriola-Headley, Jubi, 1969– author.
Title: Bound : poems / Jubi Arriola-Headley.
Description: New York : Persea Books, 2024. | Includes bibliographical references and index.
  | Summary: "Bound is a collection of poems that seeks to carve a space for Blackness and queerness in the world that isn't defined by trauma or lack, where Black and queer folks can seriously play, can create and conjure the worlds they want to live and love in"—Provided by publisher.
Identifiers: LCCN 2023038625 (print) | LCCN 2023038626 (ebook) | ISBN 9780892555789 (paperback) | ISBN 9780892555833 (ebk)
Subjects: LCGFT: Poetry.
Classification: LCC PS3601.R7225 B68 2024 (print) | LCC PS3601.R7225 (ebook) | DDC 811/.6—dc23/eng/20230927C:\Users\trod\AppData\Local\Temp\ddc.bib
LC record available at https://lccn.loc.gov/2023038625
LC ebook record available at https://lccn.loc.gov/2023038626

Book design and composition by Rita Lascaro
Typset in Sabon Light

Manufactured in the United States of America.
Printed on acid-free paper.

For Paulo—where you are, is home.

Contents

Bound

Self-Portrait as a Tidally Locked Planet

Imagine:

                 the permanent exposure

of the crust of your backside

                     to the hungry, clawing cold

                     of the Blackest of Black night.

                              Some shit you can't

just

wipe away.

                    Some weight

                         you must carry; some gusts

you best run from. The trick,

                  silly, is

less   knowing *which*,

more   *when.*

                 While on the brighter,

whiter side, you see,

        the sun's always

                    shining (oh dear! what an unsurprising

line break) and they say

            that's a blessing

        until the soil

                   cries for respite. We all need

to curl up

        our ashy toes

                 under the blanket

sometimes.

    (UGH.)

                    My most selfish impulse

        is to pluck it

        (the damned sun)

from the sky

and pop it

into my mouth.

                                        It'd burn (I KNOW)

but so does

        everything

                    I think

                    I desire

        (at first):

                    I'm used to wanting

    what I can't embrace

                                        without screaming

Mule

after Brigit Pegeen Kelly

Back in the day, way back, before alarm clocks, before sun
    dials, even, if you can believe it, when mules and men used
to speak to each other (you didn't think, you didn't presume,
    did you, that God so favored your form that They gifted only
you with the light of language), men and mules were a team,
    you see; they worked *with* each other, back when the concept
of *for* was in the manner of a gift, less an obligation, and *of* was
    a signifier for *tribe*, not *tether*. Thus it came to be that one particular
yet not-at-all peculiar man, and one particular but not-at-all peculiarly
    gifted mule had consented to be partners—collaborators, if you will—
on this great project that would come to be known early on as *agriculture*
    and later *free enterprise*, and still later, *scorched earth*. The mule of our story
was an exceedingly magnanimous sort and would counsel The Man on
    the best way to load the mule's back so that The Man could in effect
double the weight that the mule could carry. And the mule could smell
    which fields were fertile, and which were fallow, and by the tang
of last year's brome or fescue would know what day, precisely,
    to sow, to seed the fields in the season to come. And The Man, initially,
could scarce conceal his platitude, and would thank the mule profusely,
    and often, and the mule was content, because isn't that all we ever want,
in the riddle of it, to be appreciated for our art? But, over time, as any
    man will do, this particular and not-at-all peculiar one would come
to see the mule's gifts as his birthright, and by extension, the mule's craft
    as *work*. And The Man began to wonder if the mule was mule-ing
at max capacity—whether he could perhaps optimize the mule's output
    by perhaps designing a lighter and faster plow for the mule to pull, or
changing the mule's diet, so that the mule would be leaner and stronger—
    and, while not productive in and of itself, more pleasing to The Man's eye,
which couldn't hurt, could it? And the mule sensed The Man's
    arrogance, and found it annoying, to be perfectly transparent,
to such extent that the mule eventually, after much rumbling
    and rambling and grumbling and griping from The Man, said
why can't you be happy with what I give fully, freely, of my own will,
    for you? At which The Man narrowed his eyes, pursed his lips and
smacked the mule clean across the snout, with the back of his hand. *Ouch!*
    said the mule. *What the ever-negging why, my dude? Why do you mean*

to maul me? I don't know, said The Man. *Do you think it might be,* the mule
    suggested, raising a hoof to tender the throb of hurt and blood, *because
I do so much more for you than you do for me? That's fine with me, you know.
    All I've ever wanted is to be seen. A little hay, a little water, a little thanks.
I ask so little of you, if you think about it.* At which The Man cocked his
    leg and kicked the mule in the ribs. *I'm sorry, I swear, I am sorry, sorry,
sorry, I don't know what came over me, I'm having a rough day, I won't do
    you that way again, I promise,* said The Man. At which words a soupçon
of doubt crept into the mule's eyes and caused the mule's lips in turn
    to purse like lips subjected to a drought, to which The Man responded
by tendering the full weight of him, which some will argue he thought
    an offering, upon the mule's back, forcing the mule to splay on the ground.
I SAID I wouldn't do it again, The Man said, *but I can see by your face that
    you don't feel me. Where do you get off, you offal, you slough who buries
your snout in a trough, calling me small?* At this point the mule thought it best
    to be, for now, at least, silent, since The Man could never, ever be
convinced of my humanity. No matter how much I carried for him.

The Mansplaining

There are men who moor me; there are women who would
kill for me. I marvel at their loyalty. I once rubbed a dog's nose
in its own piss because MY HOME IS NOT A URINAL. I built

an elaborate wall of soup cans around it, the waste, the dog,
forced it to sit in it, the waste, the dog. At the time I failed to notice
the dog had chosen the farthest corner of the house to piss in

as if to hide its shame from me, from itself. Or I did not care. And
I'd overslept. And I was cold, to the dog, too often. (In general.) After that
the dog tried even harder to please me. What manner of godhead am I? I once

kicked in my man's door because he was unfaithful. To me—like a dog
he was true to his nature. As my foot broke through the brickle
timber, as shards of wood tore at my shin, I remember feeling free.

There's no release like rage. My first time. I cannot remember that
my cock was hard but it was. I don't know what I wanted. I know
what I wanted. I should have understood that rage would have color, and

that color would be white. I'm afraid of nothing so much as myself. I want no
more than to shed a tear when I overhear my woman making jokes with friends
at my expense. I want her pity. I want her to want to cradle my head in her lap,

to soothe me; I want her to rub my belly, to be the big spoon for the night,
for eternity. There's nothing I wouldn't give to be a child—not *again*,
so much as always. If I can't submit to you, I'll submit to my lesser reflexes.

I want so much to be bound. Save me. Save yourself.

Subphylum Crustacea

I no longer flinch when he touches me. I woke this morning
to find him gentling daybreak into the small of my back,
counter-clockwise, in rounds about the size of the wide
end of a shot-glass. In my dreaming I'd been screaming at
a small army of cockroaches, each about the width of a cast-
iron skillet, meaning to make a meal of me. In dreams they're
screams, yes, but to the waking your inner whales sound more like
whimpers. I thanked him for his kindness. Did you know that
cockroaches and blue crabs come from the same-ass subphylum,
crustacea? Both thriving despite global warming. I'll be thinking on that
next time I'm in Baltimore. From there, your crabs and cockroaches
get separated by class, not unlike how it works for humans, in life. Took
me years, years to train my skin to surrender to his touch; what blues
to think some men will cede this work, leave no trace, never know
the linger of a calloused hand. Funny how before now, I'd have
thought I wanted the biggest of every pretty trinket I could wrap
my mouth around; turns out small can be a salve, sometimes.

Adam's Daddy Issues

I've lost my

      father's

            resting face.

So humdrum, my
mourning buried
memories. Folks say
(I think) a dog can
find a buried bone
years later, just by
the whiff of it.
What skill! So
jealous. I wish I'd
learned my father's
musk; he never let
me close enough
to sniff him.

Requiem

after Victoria Chang

Died—my father, thrice: once by
his own hand, once
by mine (the second death
the physical one, beyond
the scope of this inquiry). The first death
was the day he left. By *left* I more
mean *disapparated.* By which I mean
he wasn't *gone* gone: on my morning
walk to school I'd see his
Buick parked outside the apartment
of the woman he left me for
more than I ever saw his face. By
my morning walk to school
I mean the eight blocks I walked
out of my way to pass him by.
Once I tried to slash his tires
but I only ended up in stitches. By
his tires I mean the ravage
of him from inside me. The third death
was when I tucked him inside
the folds of this poem. My mother
seems so willing to forgive. *How*,
I wonder. How?

Questionnaire I

after Bhanu Kapil

Q: Who is responsible for your mother's suffering?

A: Is there ever any answer other than
     I am? I am. From that first time I took
     another thug's aching cock in my mouth,
     cradled it in the curve of my tongue,
     sank to my knees, reached up, grabbed
     his waist to pull him deeper into me,
     suckled until I tasted his hot bitter seed,
     knew the sweat-soaked glow of triumph:
     how was this not a betrayal, proclaiming
     this moment a nursing?

Eve as Snow White as

It wasn't the apple itself I craved
though I hunger for the taste of flesh.

> It's true, I hunger for the taste of flesh;
> unseemly of a *damsel in distress*.

What a world, when a damsel in distress
can't count on the night to keep her secrets.

> Can't count on a knight to keep my secrets.
> It's the quest, in the end, for them, not the prize.

Please end your quest for this prize; these lips
will not part for your wick or your want.

> *She's all lit wick*, they'll say, *all wanton, a naught—*
> free of man's need, of God's. Leave me be.

Let me be clear: I sought freedom from God.
It wasn't the apple itself I craved.

Use As Intended

An apple can be a weapon. Why not? (There's a number of presuppositions propping up this assertion: that a thing such as an apple can have a *use*; that there is a someone or a something that made this determination—God or Adam and Eve or the serpent or Nature or the worms that relentlessly burrowed into many if not most of the apples that grew on that tree in Granny's back yard; that if there's a specific intended *use*, that there's *un*intended uses as well; that there's a value assigned to uses based on whether they are intended or unintended.) Nothing's to stop a body from grabbing an apple and hurling it at an appropriate angle and speed designed to exactly coincide with the space your head is occupying at that moment, and to connect with your noggin with sufficient impact to make you wish no bawdy had ever had the idea to use an apple as a weapon. It stands to reason that this can't be any piddly apple, though; the world's smallest apple is called the Tiddly Pomme, presumably because it makes the souls whose eyes light upon it giggle with glee. We love to tinkle over a trifle, don't we? The Tiddly Pomme, even if it was larger, couldn't possibly be a weapon because weapons have weighty names like *machete* and *shotgun* and *spear* and *semen* and *pit bull* and *patriot* and *whip* and *taser* and *brick* and *Karen*. Definitely not Tiddly Pomme. No, it would need to be a much bigger apple; the world's largest is said to be the Hokuto, a cross between a Fuji and another Japanese breed of apple you probably haven't heard of, the Mutsu. But let's get real, if you were so blessed as to stumble upon the Hokuto apple it'd likely be at a Dean & DeLuca (if they still exist) or some other upscale grocer or in a farmers market, selling for $42 per pound. Nowadays though, the ways folks toss around GMOs you probably could find a Red Delicious the size of a grapefruit if you looked long and hard enough. GMO, for those of you who don't participate in the world, is an acronym for "genetically modified organism." There's a video on YouTube of an Australian MP (which stands for "Member of Parliament") who in a speech meant to say "genetically modified organisms" but instead said "genetically modified orgasms." What a concept. It fits what we know, though, of the proclivities of humanfolk to take a thing that is, at its core, at the apex of things it can be compared to and try to make it *more*. Is this not the premise of the park? the pool? the zoo? avocado toast? The universe of things comparable to an orgasm: a sneeze. The ultimate weapon. You're damn right to worry about those maskless civilians prancing about. (Civilian: a word which shares its origins with—and this is ha ha funny—*civil*, both descendants of the Latin word which can be translated as, among other things, *affable* or *courteous*).

Folks out here worried about lawn signs and legislation and loopholes and rants and riots and insurrections. As if their every fetid breath wasn't enough to do us all in.

Breath

Strange to think I'd not thought much before now about
its drumbeat; how breath tickles the tip of my nose; how
breath ushers in memories of all the prey, the scorched prayers
I've consumed; how breath renders every bit of shredded flesh
stuck between the gaps in my history; breath's incendiary wetness,
how little droplets of breath cloud and mist and kettle-whistle
in the cold and sometimes the heat, how breath drenches my upper lip
when I wear my mask—and it's that, the mask, that's the reckoning,
the barrier between me and the world, consuming my expired
improvisations. Once upon a time I thought *this is why they rail against*
wearing their truth on their faces. Their masks, that is. It's nothing about them
wanting to be seen. As if our gaze was matte. Was matter. Oh no,
so much lighter than breath, that weight. My own ignorance is a cloak
I found in a thrift shop. My people have long known the particular structures,
I mean strictures, of breath. They've studied breath under a microscope,
cut it into splice-sized slivers with a scalpel, spread it thick over them, dared
to blanket themselves in it, in the grips of ships. It's typical to call where
they laid us, end to end, to the very last of ours, the *hold*, but I worry
you'll hear that as *embrace*, and that would be a blasphemy.

Ashes

Your thoughts & prayers
won't resurrect her
brittled bones (wood
feeds a fire, crazies
a blaze). A world watches,
mourns the loss of her
body, of our lady: *notre dame,*
like they might say
in Louisiana. There,
the church that bears
her name is one of a trinity
the sheriff's son set to ruin.
(What we call haven, he called
kindling.) When you call ours
a *black church* do you mean
to mock the char, the soot—

Naked Tarot IV (Queen of Wands)

I plant my bare feet in the gummy brown earth,
squat, plant my hands square on my hips,
and gush forth the primordial roar. I will teach you,
nonbelievers, what it means to give birth
to a verse, a nation, a movement. Learn this first:
the act of creation never doesn't require a hunger.
You are made of the same stuff you feed on—
flesh, nightshades, rumor, arroz con gandules.
And violence, too; you can always grab a stick
and summon the spirit from a snare drum or a white
canvass with the rest of them. Lesson the Second:
never let the tension ebb. Seek solace in what comes
of slinging cowshit where once nothing grew.

Little Red Riding Hood—An Alternate History

In which The Girl
marries The Wolf who
(less from hunger than
fear) nips and nibbles at
the gristle of her, bit by bit,
until she's fully reconstituted
inside his lickspittle life. There's
no room for her, much less a third.
So, desperate times, what lil' Red does is
whittle that one lean rib she never wanted
into a shiv and struts her way out of him.
(What verve! Such cockspume!) Free, not
just free but preening, bare-breasted for
all the world, bathed in his blood,
tangled up in his entrails, she asks
a passer-by for a cigarette, who's
kind enough to light it for her.
"Thanks, friend," Red says,
"What's your name?" Says
her suddenly friend-to-be,
"You can call me
Lucille. Or Lilith.
Whichever."

Renunciation

                                        I will not die for this country

                or the god

        it lies under

                        there

                        I've said it

                                I half expect the white

            page I've written this on

to rise up

                                                and smother me

                        I've not paid

my taxes since roughly

                        Sandra Bland

                                not that I'm claiming this

            is revolutionary

                        I'm pushing well past

            the middle of

                                                the middle ages

            fifty's

                        due south

                                        I'm a former

smoker and a current

                        cocksucker and

        they'll only insure my kind

                                if we consent

                to live with the sickness

                                        there's no money in

                the cure

                                (a comedian once said)

staying this side

                of whole's gonna cost me

                        $673 per month

                                        to the ministry of

        an arm and a leg

                                (possibly literally)

        on a poet's salary

                                                I'd refuse

to pay this too but

                        I will not die for this country

Machete

Listen, my loves: the path toward Liberation is thick
with bramble. It'll need to be cleared, and that's long labor,
and based on our history, who we've been, who can blame us
for not wanting to wear a yoke? To hitch our purpose to a plow?
Still, someone's got to do the work. And it might as well be
the poets. So slide, y'all, into your long long sleeves
and your thigh-high boots and grab you a machete. At first
it'll feel eel to you, that tool; it'll wriggle out your hands
like an ornery child, but I promise you, you'll hit the gist of it.
I've seen a six-year-old scamper up the full sky height
of a palm tree and, freeing herself from gravity with only
the muscles of her thighs, claim a clutch of coconuts
with a single *whack*. One for her trouble, to nurse her thirst, the rest
to market, to goddamned market. The machete's worst purpose
is to clear the path. You'll need a torch, too, to burn away
the underbrush, and thus matches, and next an accelerant.
Your rage will do just fine. As you clamber along, clearing
your way toward birth, mind you don't trip over
the helter skeletons of those who raged before you.
And resist the urge to stick a finger where it don't belong,
like an eye socket; you know damn well it's disrespectful.
What you do when you stumble upon an ancestor, is
you say—not a prayer, never a prayer—a simple Asè, then
you take a sip of your coconut water, right from the source,
in the manner of a toast. Tuck their blessing under the brim
of your belonging, then be about it. Move on. Knife your way
through the noise, the tangle, head straight for the capital –
the source of all that stench what's been wooing you all along.
Burn it. Don't think, don't blink, don't bluster; burn it all. Tender
tinder for your alms. Now, you're almost free. What comes next
is beyond the event horizon: not unknown, though unknown to you.
Between you and that moment is doubt; there's always gonna be
some simp, some whimperer slacking at the last gasp—they'll want
to grab your coconut, use the water to douse the flames. No worries.
What you'll need to do is grab your machete and whack off their hands.

Thanksgiving

I've always been the bigger
baby, if not the bigger man.
Ten pounds, twelve ounces. Just
a pound or two shy of your
average Butterball®. Wasn't
the first time I've been accused
of taking too much space. They
call this a diagnosis: so big
you can't just push me out,
so big you've got to cut me out, like
a Cancer—my rising sign, my rising
hunger. I am so much more than
what I eat; all I can stomach is
rage these days. I'll have your
fortune with some fava beans,
your privilege on the half-shell.
What a debt I owe my mother.
She let you split her open so that
I could reach for your throat.

N'Jadaka's Appeal

Hey Auntie! Can you spare me
a homeland? The one I left
didn't gift me my mother's
name. Every word I'm fighting
for: my native tongue, my immortal.

Hey Auntie. Let us carve me a tongue
to lick these wounds scriptured
on my skin. They sting, they linger,
they read as abscess—or absence;
I never learned the difference.

Hey, Auntie, maybe you could
fix your face to love me. I know
I spit chaos, but if you cut out
my tongue I will write you
a psalm, a shadow, a love song.

Hey Auntie? Why do men metaphor
mothers into countries, into tongues?
I wouldn't know. I've never had
a country. I mean, a mother.
I mean, a home. I mean, a tongue.

Caribbean Gothic | Four Women

after Nina Simone

I am a child. On the dark side of the door, four
women. Aunt Bo will wed tomorrow, the ring
around her eye a twisted gift crafted by the wrath
of the man she'll leave, in time. You'd think he misheard
the vows. *My hand in marriage*, indeed. (Or did he?)
Aunt Bo, doing her best to mute their fears. Imagine
my mother fondling Bo's shoulders, Granny cradling
Bo's big feet in her lap, them working
the weary out of Bo as best they can. Aunt Fred
off to one side, conspiring to hide Bo's split lip behind
the perfect shade of red to signal joy: shouldn't every
one? Shouldn't everyone? I've always found it funny that
my aunts all took *boy names* but left the boys behind. I am
unborn. Aunt Fred, the one my mother loved
more than her fractured tongue, falls, I mean
jumps, from a breadfruit tree, keen to be rid of me. Lands
standing on her feet. Me: a vestige. A remnant. Ain't I:
a weight. A yoke. No little girl ever survives a birth.
Forever after, or before, that girl is lost to history. What
my mother remembers is how Fred shone neon
for days after, swole *up*, turned red giant, a star in a late
stage of evolution. An unhappy ending is always
the beginning of someone else's glory. Find me any story
where there's not some someone grinning as you fall. I am
a house, my clapboard skin long since thinned
to driftwood. Not like Grandad's eyes; those pools
are Cape Cod coast in winter, echoing tones
you'd think they could not know. You just know

old G was a heartbreaker. Once. No, this hue shows
more like Granny's crusted feet, still mimes a purpose
but threatening to quit any minute.

                                        —I am

four rooms square, this house. My front room, too, had
purpose, once, to welcome well-heeled, sleek-soled
folk, let y'all cast your tired tails on the settee a spell,
spill some good tea, sip Earl Grey (octaned with a mite
of the finest whiskey) from brittle china cups shined
'til their flower patterns dulled like the silk ones
in Granny's hair, nibble on some sweet bartered
for a lick of laundry or bought with next week's
meat budget. (Rice and peas it'll be. Again.) Nowadays,
no one ever tips through that front door. Granite steps,
ground to nubs like Granny's toes, too treacherous
for slick-souled Sunday scrubs to navigate. Now it just
plays host to a cat and a log of *coulda beens*: Grandad
thirsting in the room to the left, scouring the street below,
watching his neighbors warrior on to better lies. Granny's room
looking over the pigs and their slop. They each stay
mute in their corner—only meet in the kitchen, kerosene
powering the stove, lighting their slack faces as well, the space
between them thickening like gravy, the silences relieved by
an occasional *hiss* and *pop* of lard in Granny's cured and crusted
cast-iron skillet. Or when she lets fall droplets of water on the bottom
of the iron, sure it runs murdering hot as she presses and starches
Grandad's collars. What for, I'll never guess. Granny was always
the working one. From the moment I could speak her name
until the day she died, she never looked to me like she was *loved*.
I could tell you that I loved her. But until the day she lost

her voice Granny always said *I cannot STAND a fucking liar*. I am
a fucking liar. When my mother asks whether *this poem is about me*
I'll smile while side-stepping the question like I've done so many
men I didn't love. She deserves a better son: one who is unwilling
to language the living. I'll use words like *cypher* and *composite* and cite
creative license in the hope of straight confounding her into silence.
And I'll succeed. I'll need you to take it on faith when I say I can't
love any mother the way they deserve and yet bare the truth of me.

Jack

The summer I turned eleven they sent
(read: banished) me to live (die) with Granny.
She, who'd lost six kids before Dad, was bent
on saving or saging or scaring me

square, so she summoned the obeah man
to read my cards for two bottles of Jack,
a blunt, & twenty bucks U. S. He drank
the first bottle right then—his jaw got slack

but that didn't slow his slick. (The long con
had bled Granny before, not with a knife
but with hope.) I caught the jack of spades on
the flop; for her that was it—he'd blessed my life.

Granny's thin lips turnt, let go of the grim
but *I* know a high-jack when I see him.

Ode to the Lone Star State

after Greg Abbott

For me it's more than portion sizes; love
tastes best when it's deep-fried. Someone said
once *love is lard* and I believe them. Pickles
and Twinkies subjected to the same God-
damned transmutation. The triumph of oil
in all things. In Texas if you ask for your
steak *well-done* they'll smile all the while
they burn it on purpose. To teach you.
Boo you if you can't take a joke—the Texas
state flag includes a single white star floating
on a regiment of blue, perpendicular to two
Texas-sized lies. I mean lines. Bravery, purity:
a cross-section of the national group-think
blown up to Texas-sized distortions. Everyone
knows Texas neighbors are the politest, even
the ones would shiv you in church or
in the halls of the state Capitol. Texas
folk can always spare a *good morning*
or a *how ya doin'* while walking the dog
or shopping for ammunition. The Texas heat
is disconnected from the rest of the grid.
Our survival instincts tell us when to show 'em,
when to fold our faith into a gush of mustered
thoughts and prayers. The triumph of *I* in all things.

Questionnaire II

after Bhanu Kapil

Q: **Describe a morning you woke without fear.**

A: Y'all act like poetry can fix the world?
Show. Me. When. I don't know, friend. I don't think
I'm enough to save the world. (That last crack

is a misdirection. I don't believe
the world's worth saving.) Didn't know until
this morning when I Googled it to write

my artist statement what *Afropessimist*
means and not real sure I grasp the mass
of the term but it's starting to smell like

my Granny's blanket—like mothballs
and myths though Granny's long gone,
swaddling the me lying belly-down sofa-bound

round 3AM, snacking on surreality TV and
trans fats, thinking my most revolutionary imperative
might be to die by the hand I dealt myself.

Twilight

after Craig Santos-Perez

The only thing I truly fear
is daybreak. By this I mean
I fear what the day holds for me.

I fear I'll be walking down some shady lane
when the trees have had enough, rip their roots
from the oil-soaked soil and aching

haul their harrowed husks my way, wailing
through the miles, *why?* I fear the birds will
spy me in the park (what if the pigeons are

in league with the grittier birds, the crows
and cardinals and cockatoos?) and collude
to peck the flesh from me. I fear the ocean

will call due the note on the land it's ceded us,
the land we dredged, we dragged from its bosom,
like a child, from a mother, cage-bound and

drown us for nonpayment. I fear the fishes
will form a school to teach their children
to hate us, like wet refugees might do.

I fear the extant planets will come to save
their sister. And though I don't speak the brook's
babel, I know they call me *boneyard*—

Ways to Spot an Invasive Species

Challenge it to a word association game.
Say *goat* and if it counters with
cheese instead of *curry* you might have
an overgrowth. Say *banana* or *bay* right quick
and wait for *leaf* or silence to follow.
Say *ferment* and if its first thought
is not *kimchi or pig's feet* but
craft beer, make sure you pull
that puckish weed out by its roots.
Ask where you can get the best local
roti. Mofongo. Empanadas. (If you don't
know the answers yourself, might be
you who's out of place.)
It must be said, though:
these weeds grow from seeds
that float on the winds
of whisper campaigns; they'll do
what they must to resist being pulled. So:
try never to munch on your chicharrones
while bird-watching in any park. Wash
the curry stains from your fingers before
you fall asleep round an Ivy. Don't ferment
anything within two hundred clicks of a pistol.
When you go jogging, for the love
of a return trip, mind you don't slip
through the cracks. Mind you don't barrel
into a cracker. Mind your manners. Mind your
mouth. Mind your melanin.

Haiku (On Appropriation)

The only white folk
who may enter Black Heaven
is Teena Marie.

Declaration

I hold these moods like embers on my tongue: that *text* is
a subset of *language*. That language is a mode of binding.
That my fists are bound in language. That by *language*
I mean picaresques and platitudes and glances sideways
and downward, this twisted whisper in my bones, the searing
of which courses through me like blood, which perhaps
constitutes the substance itself, my blood. That when I say
my fists are bound in language I mean you to understand that
my fists stay clenched, whether or not you perceive each
discrete finger extended. That you should never understand
my proffered hand as a gesture of welcome. That *my* should be
heard in a mode of accrual, not possession. That I have given you
everything, every clue you'd need to believe that you ought not
ever hear *you* as appeal or accusation but rather a branding. That
you've branded yourself. That no manner of branding can purge
you of your history. That by *history* I mean *acts of war*. That *I* is I and I.

Once

after Bhanu Kapil

Q: How have you prepared for your death?

A: I used to want to be a landmark, a point of departure for the driftless, the ramblers. See: Malcolm. See: Jimmy. See: Nina. See: Billy. But then I thought about what you—or what we call this roiling foment to foment— took from them. Insisted of them. And I realized I'd rather be dissed by history. I don't even want to be a hashtag. A hashtag is fireworks in July; it sparks and starbursts for a millimoment, then it fades. You'll remember it, down the road, but hazy; its lines and contours will never again come into focus. Nor a footnote; I don't aim to explain a damn thing to anyone. That's been my life up to now, see? Just unsee me. Train your gaze elsewhere. Miss me with your collusions of Beaux Arts lecture halls and colosseum naming rights. I bear enough of a lode, thank you very much. I've got precious little of what you'd call *ambition*: to breathe, for a few more todays. To splay naked in the sun, on a beach free of plastic. To taste your grandma's signature dish, whatever that is. To feel at home in my own body, no matter its warp, its weft. To know what *home* is. I can't see a way out of this. Once, a poet suggested that if I was stuck in a poem I could insert the word once and go from there, see where once takes me. To wit: there is no *out*. Another said that all that's ever left of any age is poetry and architecture, the one crafted of stone, the other, not. I could never have been an architect; I cannot render in hardscape what it means to endure.

Queer Fan Fiction—Frida & Josephine @ La Casa Azul

Josephine slays, for days, lays
the rhythmic glyph of her across

the cool saltillo floor, coaxes her
toes into a perfect en pointe, tucks

the world behind her eyes, says
cast me however you will. Frida forgets

every fickle bit of man or metal
that ever pierced her, drops to her

brittle knees—her hands, too, fall, unable
to resist the pull of gravity, to Josephine's

errant belly. There Frida lazy traces
circle after flawless circle; Josephine

giggles, forgets to taut like she's
expected to. Her breath expands—

rises, rises to meet the hardened
tips of Frida's paint-stained fingers.

I've never met a canvas that would not
respond to touch, Frida whispers.

Josephine begins to sing: *wanting you*
is my offence / you have all the evidence /

now I wait for you to sentence me . . . death,
Frida thinks, death by a thousand

blisses. Frida reads like a book
to Josephine, who lifts a single

finger, says everything she needs
to with a hook: *Come.*

RESOLVED: I will no longer apologize

for the way I drape my cellulite over
my belt buckle, or your arm rest, or the way
I toss my drawers off at the slightest provocation.
For the way I run my tongue along the underside
of a foreskin, much the same as I run the flat
of my palm along the knife edge of the flat
sheet on a bed well made. For singing all
the wrong lyrics to a song I made up on the spot.
For slathering hot sauce on every plate
you slide under my nose, after I've tasted it.
For looking downward, toward the swing
of the pendulum. For not meeting your gaze.
For the country. For the wars. For the flags.
For my loose hips, my wide ass, my wise-ass
cracks, for waxing my ass crack. For wanting it
to slide in easy, and deep. For deep thinking
about anything other than whatever you are
blathering the fuck on about. For Mondays.
For not yet having found life on other planets,
or a tee shirt that that makes you see in me
a buck. Better yet, a buck fifty. For napping
in the middle of your pearl-encrusted scurries.
For not believing in God. For God.

Goddam Cento

And when I descended to the valleys and the plains
God was there also, *God*, again, all *up* in the Kool-Aid.
Antic God, aphrodisiac God, without one friend,

another gorgeous thing that should not have happened.
(My God, why did I turn my eyes upward as if He were
weightless? A little flying God Almighty in the sky,

the beating of the wings, unheard.) All day I keep hearing
the fighting in the valley. Dear God for whom I am
one green marble: why do you hide behind your mask

(the sun and stars)? Show yourself. You lied to me,
all these years. I do not mean to be fatalistic:
if to be a God means to consider the fact of my own

demise, what I once was and where I have been—a body
that turns toward openness, fantasy—then I am God,
we are God, whose beloved breath becomes (at last) our own

God Responds . . . to the Proust Questionnaire

The Proust Questionnaire has its origins in a parlor game popularized (though not devised) by Marcel Proust, the French essayist and novelist, who believed that, in answering these questions, an individual reveals [their] true nature.
   —Vanity Fair

Where the typical journalistic interview tailors questions to the particular qualities of a subject, the Proust questionnaire's unchanging ritual confers a special kind of prestige, granting the tastes, opinions, and preferences of celebrities a timeless, philosophical appeal. Whether you're a philosopher or a sitcom actor, your value is affirmed by the mere fact that you've been asked the questions at all.
   —The New Yorker

I. In Queen's Park in Bridgetown stands a baobab tree that's abided nigh on ten centuries—rooted before the rise of the great Kingdom of Benin, struggled upward toward the light before Mansa Musa built mosque the first in Timbuktu. Once, companion grasses and grains of sand strew themselves upon the ground around her, *la baobab*, a gesture toward fealty; a grove of bearded figs (from which the island takes its name) stood sentinel. Now her nearest neighbor's a car park and her once-fecund foothold is today an encasement of concrete, but she's no less regal for it. The typical myth would have you believe it was chance landed her on distant shores, an errant seed carried away by the currents of the day. No, no; *chance* is a battered concept we old and wizened understand is nothing but lazy metaphysics. Imagine, rather, her sisters gathering up all the strength of their various branches of history and hurling that embryonic flash three thousand miles across the ocean, so her cousins would someday recognize those shores as a place you could make a home. Despite the concrete encasing your feat.

II. My pronouns *they/them*, my gender
       a comet, a cosmic snowball begging

   to melt, a crush of gas and rock and dust
       in orbit around what warms me. Round

my fists I spool thin ribbons of flamingo
        scissored from the spectrum of sunburst.

III. In the beginning, there was possibility. There sparked, between what
was not and what now is, a moment, where anything might happen,
any splendid wretched thing. Let me metaphor it for you: the tabby
might've been rotting dead inside the box, or knitting a scarf for its
auntie, or wailing away on a tambourine or trombone, or dead-set
on clawing its way out, or the cat might not have been a cat at all, it
could've been a banana leaf or an elephant or a typhoon or a cyborg
or the box might have held only light and air. It's not the moment
before you take your first hit of your very first spliff that's the shit;
it's the moment it hits you, when you're overwhelmed by the flood,
when you begin to understand how much you really don't. How do
you ever recover that high? How can you ever un-know descent?

IV. An unadulterated (HA!) list of the ones of you I've truly loved
(each name of which also appears on the ongoing list of folks I've
thoroughly fucked)—

- Jesus, that melodramatic scamp. The cross was his idea, you
  know. For the allegory. In case you didn't suss it out, our boy was
  a poet. He just didn't trust you to weed between the lines. I mean,
  read between the vines. I stay stunned that in churches all across
  this rock you've bleached his skin and darkened the wood when
  it was quite the flip way round; the pulp of the cross was pinkish
  pale and your messiah's skin was ebony.

- I so longed to see through Van Gogh's eyes. I used to whisper
  sticky sweet somethings to him as he painted his age and he told
  his friend Paul what I told him and that thankless rutted fuck told
  old Vin *your ears don't work right, you should get new ones* and
  my darling took Paul transliterally.

  (I've had my share of scrapes with pricks named Paul.)

- Nina would have none of me—she was the most demanding, of
  herself above everyone else. I wanted to worship her like she

39

deserved to be worshipped. Like I wanted to be worshipped. But I could not feed her need enough. Miss Simone legit had a bone to moan about her entire liminal life.

IX. In the western highlands of Guatemala, where the volcanoes whip the groundwaters into an obscene heat, and the local boys boil their blues in lava-fueled pools to prove their mental, there's a city the Maya call Xelajú. And in this city there's a young girl, barely skirting the edge of seventeen—let's call her

La Michelada.

She was born to a mother who wanted to love her. But the world being what it is, she struggled to be herself. The mother, the daughter. Her father wanted a boy. Her father insisted she embrace a boy. Her father tried to force a boy into her, but she would not. She would not. Oh, her stunning funk, her wondrous runtish. You know how the story goes—she'll end up fending, scavenging. Her mettle will net her dependents, months younger than her. She'll sell whatever she can stand to let men lay their hands on. She'll bloom into a thing that means to be more than what surrounds it.

X. Can you perceive your edges? Do you bleed and blend into the surrounding painscape? Some days I feel like my axiomatic sofa's grafted onto my ass. Not that what you call a *sofa* is where I rest. Not that I've ever known rest. The "day" they say I did was an anxious one for me. I reconsidered every poem I'd ever made. What and why the aardvark? the antelope? the artery? the asterisk? I began at what I told myself was the beginning. I have no sense of where I end. I, anamorph, I parallax. What manner of mirror would one select to reflect the universe back unto itself?

XI. Once, I strode down Whitechapel Road, as up from the gutters, or so I dreamed, tufts of turmeric wafted and drifted, cimarrón, toward the tip of my tongue, like dandelion seeds blown nomad by a wildling child, and catches of cumin tore at my nostrils, flared them like lust, parting them wide, they, wanting more than they could possibly take, and everywhere around me men in tunics, robes

of spun sunshine, bright as weathered wool, walked, arms locked,
clung, sung to each other in satin baritones, let fingers lay lovered on
shoulders, claimed kisses as warriors do, as if they full knew the cost
of softness and chose to pay it nonetheless, tendering in full view of
the glory of a shop sign that read *Bangladeshi Curry Centre* and all I
kept thinking was *which God is theirs?*

XII. That Langston hangnail scribbled some vicious verse—*without one*
friend, he said, *alone in my purity*, he said. That fucktoast. The
nerve. Though he might've got it righter than most. And mine and
Hughes' views on purity and poetry are close.

XIII.   I am
           a void
           I'm ever
           swelling

XIV. No paradox here—Blackness

        is never an absence. No gesture's ever gone, ever *not*; if it
is, it'll be and has been. No matter what the physics say—I am the
ochre and umber wind-stripped from every marble mannequin;
I'm every heavy leaden curse you've ever vespered to the wind,
a blowball filament meant to take root wherever it lands, rout
whatever sative species it encounters.

XV. consider yourself a mountain
                              formed in the first of the fires & fissures
that shaped this place
                  yet I, then, must needs be
                          the river, simple, rippling, true

     & simply course around you
                    or

                            if it better serve you
cast yourself the godhead
            yet I will sing your sin   your wedded excess

what faith can swaddle you safe

have you not heard   the gospel chorus

I shall not be moved

you   vestige   apparition   nothing

dust   soon swept away

XVI. You must see by now that I'm agnostic about the outcome. I can't
tell you how this ends. Not *won't*; *can't*. I've never been one to
gamble; I cast no die that you can pin your sorry lot on. Chance is
a sucker's bet, every time. This bitch of a situation was created by
y'all who did, and y'all who don't. Ask yourself whose rules you're
beholden to. If some seedy bearded greedhead wants to hoard
enough Bitcoin to mount a cockrocket straight to Mars, who's to
stop 'em? The baobabs are dropping dead, splitting time along
their shriveling spines, not one by one as you'd expect but in some
wicked chorus line, like it's goddam 42nd Street up in here. If I won't
intercede, if I let their thirsty wood chips fall where they may, then
please understand that where and when your teeth secede from your
mealy mouth is of little consequence to me. I won't lose a minute
over you.

XVII. Think of *empire* as a board game. There are two sets of rules. Rules
the first: if you must go, make sure you go gentle. Get in line, in
order of might. Raise your hand before you riot. Don't you dare
nod off in the middle of this sentencing. Pay your taxes right after
you pay your tithes. You know they renew every year, right? You're
never *done* done, humdrum. You've been in arrears since before you
were born. Are you listening? The future's a privilege, not a rite;
we'll let you know when you've earned it.

XVIII. Y'all keep pandering to the (d)rafters with that stacked deck if you
want to.

XIX. There's a boy, maybe eight or nine years old, set out on his front stoop, reading a book—*The Autobiography of Malcolm X*. (He can't barely imagine what he's reading but that don't daunt him; this summer he'll end up reading it cover to cover, twice.)

The sun's a screaming tangerine in the sky.

A car speeding down the street screeches to a freeze in front of the boy. Its *screeeeeech* sounds like bleating, puts the boy in the mind of a panicked animal. Looming. Dangerous. The man in the driver's seat of the car turns to the woman in the passenger seat of the car and punches her in the face. Three times, in rapid succession, *boom boom boom*. (Years on, the boy, no longer a boy, forever that boy, will recollect each punch as accompanied by an audible boom, low and rumbling, troubling and trembling the earth around it, like thunder, like an edifice imploding.) The boy in the back seat of the car is no older than the boy on the stoop. In a single fluid movement, or so it seems to the boy on the stoop, the man in the driver's seat retracts his arm, turns back to the steering wheel, and screeches off, as suddenly as he appeared.

XX. Years on, in the myth the boy will wish into insistence, the man's fist freezes, millimeters from the woman's nose, blocked by some unseen force. The boy on the stoop raises his left hand from his lap; the book he's reading slow-moes to the ground, spawning an audible *boom* as it hits. A sudden soundtrack backs the boy, black and blue music racing toward crescendo. The boy, his expression the square root of inscrutable, stretches his arm toward the man, works his fingers, and then, in a single, fluid movement, twirls his fingers into a fist of his own making. Being better versed in fairy tales and looney tunes than in life, the boy expects that the man's fist will first stiffen to stone, then crumble to dust that floats away like petals from a flower on a windy day. You and I, of course, know better. The man's hand is crushed and twisted into a mess of ripped skin and burst flesh and torn cartilage and broken bones and blood, blood everywhere. The man's scream pierces the swollen air; he's a panicked animal. Looming. Dangerous.

XXI. Did you know that the word *tangerine* comes from the 18th century *tangerino*, signifying (and this is wild, child) *a person from Tangier*? Not at all the same root as *tangent*, which comes from the Latin *tangere*, *to touch*.

XXII. I love a good tangent

XXIII. I marvel at the middling things, the almost-missed: how on hundreds of corners in front of hundreds of corner stores, hundreds of men in ranging stages of inebriation are right now pounding down draughts, and dominoes on tables like they're lashes on backs. They only want to be ~~heard~~, these men. How what they call a table—a square of rain-warped plywood high-wiring atop a long-retired oil barrel—never flips from the force of this lift, this kick. How the dominoes shift, nervous, yet never straying too far from where they've been slapped into line. They know better than to protest. Dominoes is a game of balance, of restraint, of bounding toward the edge of a raging cataract and tumbling over instead of turning around and spraying those pursuing you with your graven verse. Wives, in peacetime, curse these men for not coming home to them. Not that they *want* them home—they've had all they can take of those crusty feet ripping their sheets and shins to shreds. But they want them to *want* to be.

XXIV. In wartime mothers of sons curse their luck, wish they'd borne daughters. They forget they too were daughters, once.

XXV. Y'all let your cities swallow stories whole.
Who among you knows whether Sly's alive
or five feet under? FYI, the last

reported sighting: sweating in a tent
off Sunset, the latter half of twenty-
eleven. But who'd even give a good

me-damn, if you couldn't package his fight
as a ninety-minute pilot? Like, who
among y'all longs to follow a subplot?

44

XXVI.   I once eavesdropped on a workshop wherein a person with pale-
        ish pink skin and ebony hair that ended in a flatline just below
        her earlobes who was known to slog her way around a verse said
        in response to a question (not directed to her, I might add) *I hate
        questions* and it was as if the room became a vacuum, no friction
        coefficient, and all the poets' jaws dropped at the exact same
        speed and hit the floor at the exact same moment and the boom
        was inaudible depending on what you perceive *hearing* to be but
        nonetheless that day that crack shook the foundations of the craft.
        She (the person) made few friends that day, believe you me. That she
        made any at all is perhaps my greatest failing.

XXVII.   I long to be
                    thunderstruck
                    sting of open hand
                    landing   full-on cheek

XXVIII. No, lower.

XXIX.   I can crack a joke and a whip with equal dexterity.

XXX.   Did you hear the one where the one who plays the wife asks the one
        who plays the husband, *what would you do if we won the lottery?
        I'd take my half,* says the husband, *and I'd leave you before you
        could say "inheritance tax." Great!* says the wife. *I won twenty
        bucks last night. Here's ten. Stay in touch!*

XXXI.   What if touch was
                    a victimless crime
                    Would anyone
                    touch me then

XXXII. I once mused that if we knew who baked the first sweet potato
        pie we should make their name a day of the week and some critic
        (aren't you all) suggested I was speaking rhetorically or ironically or
        hyperbolically or some other such shit-sense but what if—and hear
        me out—what if I wasn't? There's a cast-in-bronze goddess set dead-
        center in the atrium of the Metropolitan Museum of Art and I'm

just saying what if it was a for-true bronze goddess what was hopped
up on pedestals? What if her name was Ma'khia? Or Breonna? How
would your lives materially change? Is it worth the flight to find out?
When I'm being hyperbolic you better-well know you'll know it.
When I cast your sorry lots into the bellies of whales and ride your
pencil skyscrapers into the blood-flooded mud and side-eye your
shithole cities into pillars of salt—

XXXIII.   At the birth of each new day
              I wake with one wish: to flay
              Myself, free of form—
              of *boy*, of *body*, of *bloat*

XXXIV. Once, you were—not free, not stout of wing like the eagles, but,
though bound to earth, given to roam beyond the barbed-wire
words this bird pelted you with. It happened while you were
watching—now that's some twisted magic trick. The coin's never not
been there, between these sticky fingers; you just didn't see it. What
a fuss, learning to listen with your eyes. HEY! My alibis are up here,
m'dear! But what you ought to be watching is my sleight-of-hand
job.

XXXV. Like all true gauds my revelations please me, until I parse the
implications.

Lost In Translation

The names are always Biblical—Tienda *Santa Maria* or *San Miguel* or *La Fe,*
which does not translate into "store of the uglies," I have too late learned.
A single letter will split a mouth into a moth, a horse into a hose, a *now* into
a *no.* (If ever there was a gendered confessional, this must be it.) Whatever
you call it—a tienda, a bodega, a corner store—just know I'm shopping there
because the plátanos are never less than a day past ripe, which is when
they're the sweetest, right? And no one commits the venial sin of trimming
the fat off the chicharrones. Mis abuelos wash them down with Modelo Negra
while squatting out front on their milk-crate stools, playing dominoes. Buen
provecho, I say, in passing. All nod. One smiles. I feel proud. I don't stumble.

Tell me you're a poet without *telling* me you're a poet.

once is my favorite word | if i read your rime & my response is DAMN
it means ive stopped breathing | for a minute | FUCK means all the air
has fled my body | whoosh | thats ONOMATOPOEIA right there |
silence means an alien army has descended & with their (of course)
superior alien technology suctioned 97% of the atmosphere into one
billion phallus shaped receptacles each the combined length & girth
of the 1987 los angeles lakers starting lineup & left us earthbound
flora & fauna to fight over the remaining scraps | (there is capitalism
on betafuck-12 also) | i know nothing about basketball | but the image
was too hard to ignore | so | i never expect to make a dollar
from my craft | if i wanted to make money id write fiction | heres one |
a fiction that is | once upon a time there was a bard who never once
noted or quoted the ocean in any verse theyd ever scribbled | ever |
i only ever wear black to my readings | my favorite pastime is discovering
the etymology of words | lets investigate the etymology of maroon |
its so much more than a color | trust | i write all my text messages
with FULL GODDAM PUNCTUATION | tired of yall | shoot | i write
my riddles with absolutely none | none youd recognize anyway |
i change form & shape at will |

i
          will
put
          1
                    bootylicking
word
          on
                    each
                              nipplesucking
                                        line

48

fight

          me

a poem a day is the only prescription i can afford to fill | i can fall in love
with any physic without ever actually receiving you | write any line that
makes me laugh & GUARANTEED ima let you hit. this. | HARD |
fuck around & make me bust a gut & see if i dont make you bust a nut |
im ~~not~~ proud of that last shit but | the fruit was hung low | real low |
like my balls | i cant stop | which is to say | i stay tryna
make you love me | always | you cant ever hurt me worse than
i hurt myself | looking in the mirror this morning | to me the phrase
black lives matter contains 3 verbs | the only time i dont feel alone is

here

        now

black (v.)

*a speculative definition for the forthcoming
Oxford Dictionary of African American English*

To vanta. To haint. To hiss
and spittle. To soar into
a pirouette then drop into
a twerk. To *werk*. To rub
petroleum onto an eager
new moon. To moonlight,
to mythscape, to reach. To render,
to vendor. To give the last
of what you never had to your sister
for a whiskey run. To cornbread,
to cornrow. To dread, to lock,
to pop, to sizzle. To riddle.
To chicken
and biscuit and waffle. To
greens. To green, to grow,
to watermelon, to summon
miracles from the reluctant dirt.
To linger way past sundown
in the park, in the dance hall,
in the back yard after all
the crabs done been cracked
and sucked dry. To Baltimore.
To Detroit, to New Orleans,
to Chicago, to *Atlanta*.
To the Bronx and Brooklyn
and Queens. To Oakland.
To Accra. To homecoming,

to homegoing, to going
apeshit for go-go. To jazz,
to trap, to tribal vibe,
to reggae, to calypso,
to salsa, to spice, to rhythm.
To *Bitches Brew*, to *Kind of Blue*, to blues,
plural. To dime, to lime, to wine.
To instrument, to strum,
to ride that high note, to slap
that bass line, to slide
electric across the asphalt
to *Before I Let Go*. To maze,
to faze, to coin
the phrase that blazes.
To stunt, to front, to flow,
to glow, to know.
To *Everyday People*.
To everyday people.
To quiet
storms. To freak,
to geek, to rile, to *chile*,
to mother the child
that's got (or not), the block,
the neighborhood,
the universe. To history.
To *all y'all*. To shout, in
a ring, in a church, in
formation. To *Formation*.
To lay, to slay, to never
come to play. To play.

"I *got* my education" Or Mix-n-Match Thesis Titles

	Epistemology		This Pot of Oxtails[1]
	Ontology		'Cancel Culture'
	Teleology		A Living Wage
A	Hermeneutics		Gender Fluid
An	Metaphysics	*of*	Afro Sheen™[2]
The	Archive		Late Capitalism
	Lexicon		Corner Stores[3]
	Taxonomy		The Dozens[4]
	Semiotics		*Good Times*[5]
	Pedagogy		A Jail Cell
	Deconstruction		'Political' Poetry
	Aesthetics		Gettin' By[6]

---

1 Have you ever rubbed, just *scrubbed* a thing til it was putty in your hands? Beat then teased the meat with the slow roll simmer? Had your lover watering at the mouth for a taste of what you could deliver? No? Then maybe sit this one out, stick to what you know.

2 Spread it thick. Slick it. We wanna peep that sheen from outer space. Smack it. Flip it! Reverse it, rub it down. Yo yo! I need my damn durag.

3 "Bodegas" is also acceptable.

4 As in: "YO, you laid that Afro Sheen™ on so thick aliens can see you from outer space! Smell your ass too. Look like your head melting."

5 Now, I'm not trying to be an ass—you know Florida's character *made* that show what it is—but didn't you ever once wonder why Thelma's hair was always *laid* and it look like Florida never even heard of Afro Sheen™? Just *dry*. I mean, like, couldn't they share product?

6 An expansive term, the praxis of which may include but is not limited to spades games; fish frys; gospel choirs; house music; Aretha's ouevre, excepting a brief period in the 1980's; Luther's "A House Is Not a Home," which exists alongside and outside what folks call *time*; backyard bounty harvested from two inches of sand ("come get you summa these tomatoes before they get too soft"); various conjugations of the verb *to be*; line dances; slow-walking in any city along any boulevard named after MLK; Q-Tips®, specifically (no off-brands); Vaseline®, specifically (NO OFF-BRANDS); lotion, to taste; purchasing any product, in person, preferably in bulk, from Sally Beauty® Supply; and, in general, refusing to cease to exist.

Banjo

It's commonly understood, though they mayhem the history, that the earliest of us to be grafted onto this stolen land carried naught with us but our scars, and our memories. Often, those were one and the same. But when they weren't— when they weren't, we remembered our memories and birthed spitting iterations of what had been, back home, into what was needed, here. Context, as ever, was key. The Banjo, for example—a great-great-great-great-unto-the-Juneteenth-power-great grandchild of an instrument of exchange, born of independent minds in Senegambia and in the land of Wassoulu music, too, with cousins in Persia and China and Japan and Morocco but none to speak of from the lands of the folks whose offspring stay trying to claim it nowadays for their own. It's a matter of conjecture whether they stole it from us because they understood its power, or because they didn't. What we know, what is engraved upon our every bone: the exercise of pleasure as revolution. The incantatory vapors it raises, they steady us. We breathe, deep, for all those what couldn't.

Eddie, or Ecstasy

1.

Take this pill and swallow it, Eddie says
and you do as you're told; Eddie runs
the plays and you're no one's player. This boy's
backstory can't be beat: son of the son
of the son of the stiff who "built" Kentucky's
last bourbon distillery, though the crime
in this myth is how Great Gramps won it—
it's true, on a dare; the dare itself, time's
dulled and dimmed. Cue Eddie, heir apparent
snuffed out, thanks to his rank faggotry.
I wears my cuntry on my tongue, Eddie
purrs in his butter-whipped Southern drawl;
we queers know that *oh!* is a sound we'd best
leave to girls clutching pearls and bedroom brawls.

2.

Eddie's that friend who'll scream *fuck the rich*
in the face of old money, then fuck old
money's son face down in old money's bed.
I love to hear 'em scream 'oh! Daddy!' Eddie
laughs, still counting the grift he's lifted from
young money's wallet. But here's the stunner—
Eddie, he always splits his take with you,
fifty-fifty. And you'll take that gift and
spend like you earned it. Eddie did, for sure.
Eddie's some kinda looker; his eyes are
brown as any fertile earth, and dead-set
closer than any Renaissance master
would ever cast in stone or on stage or
in love. Plus: his head's shaped like a trapezoid.

3.

Though Eddie's no stunner he's loyal
to the last: he'd kill for you, and you have
never been one to dance alone. So you
swallow the pill and he swallows too and
 you wait. And wait. *I'll be back,* Eddie says,
and it hits you that this is the end
of your friendship. Eddie's at last seen the light.
He's a landmark, a star; you're not even
a satellite. At best you're space junk.
A cast-off. Driftless. Drifting. You know now
how you hate Eddie, how you need him.
Eddie leaves you sitting on his shredded
tweed sofa and he walks out the door and
you want to cry but don't really know why.

4.

Have you once thought of tweed, even
once, as a drug? As a slut, as a tease,
as a marvel? Once, on a train, you were
wearing your cut-off high-slit denim shorts
that paid mute tribute to your thick boy-thighs
when a man (also wearing shorts) chose to
sit right next to you; his thick hairy limb
pressed into yours and each one of those hairs
stroked you senseless and though there was room for
this man to pull his thigh away it seemed
that he was digging deeper into you
and when your fingers stroke that tweed you know
to stroke that tweed like it's a lover's skin.
Like it's a wanton field that craves your plow.

5.

Is this your skin? Where does it begin?
Is this your textured flesh? You grope your
Doppelgängered kin like you've found your own
hard-rock anthem for the last of first times;
you're combing every undiscovered place
to learn what gets you off. In this here and
how, the pain of a prick straining against
its prison of pants is somehow a sanction.
A stranger in the hallway stops and stares;
Eddie left the door wide open and you
couldn't care less. *Ecstasy?* they ask, more
state, matter-of-fact, like the weather or
the red stripe down the middle of our map.
This moment known to them, old, familiar.

6.

You, you . . . nod; the muscles we use to speak
need more blood to function than you can spare.
Oh! I see Miss Molly's come calling, says
Eddie. He muscles past his neighbor, pulls
up behind you, rubs your scalp with the nibs
of his fingers. Your eyes roll back into
your dreams, your once upon a time. Now his
hands float to your ears, loving them between
his lingers. *How's that feel,* he asks; all you
can manage in answer is *mmmmmm.* Eddie's
hands drop down to your shoulders, kneading all
of the locked, the awkward out of you and
you feel so light—you'd float clean away if
Eddie's hands weren't an anchor. A calling.

7.

Eddie lets his hands wander beyond your
decents; between each of his thumbs and
index fingers he grasps a plump nipple.
Eddie rubs and rolls and pinches and tweaks
them in some exquisite combination—unlocks an
ooooooooo that morphs into *uuuunnnnhhh* and then into
a gawping silence. You spread your legs wide
(you know why), reach back with your hands, grab him
round his waist and tilt your head up and
suddenly you're kissing, and this kiss is
your surrender. You will your self to him—
take this body and eat it, my body,
which I give freely unto you. Eddie
stops kissing you, stops stealing your soul.

8.

You wonder if you said the words aloud,
but no—Eddie lets go of your nipples,
your live wires (and for however many
aeons pass you fret that you might never
know that ecstasy again), hops over
the sofa, drops to his knees between yours,
works, wills his hands under your waistband,
pulls; your hips without direction rise up
in offering. Eddie slides your shorts right
over your high tops and off and your cock,
slick at the tip, stands, exposed to Eddie
and the world (*is the door still open?*) and
Eddie whispers *beautiful* and you, you
believe him. Eddie leans forward, kisses it.

9.

Eddie kisses the tip, not your eyes, though that
is where the waters gather. And that feels wrong
but also right. Eddie undoes the buttons
of his own shorts and there's his own fat, pure
pride and all you want is Eddie in you.
Eddie slides you forward and your hips are
liquid, presses the tip of his pride against
your walls and you push back, a good boy
begging to be breached. *Is . . . this . . . what you want?*
Eddie asks. And it's important here
to be fair to Eddie, to remember
he doesn't ask like he's a porn star in
the thick of a shoot, or like he's owed it,
or even like a man. *Is this what you want?*

Letter to My Nether Regions

Dear Low-T: Dear tea-stained teeth: Dear teabags
under my eyes: Dear eyes (dear precious whetstone,
dear refraction of light): Dear ribboning skin:
Dear burnt sugar hue: Dear ancestors—dear Taíno,
dear Kalinago, you good and peaceful folk; dear Ashanti:
Dear Ghana: Dear Togo: Dear Benin: Dear Benin-bronze
face: Dear cheekbones: Dear spread-nose: Dear thick-lips:
Dear buck, uncut: Dear shower, dear grower: Dear upward
arc: Dear low and loose: Dear freedom swing: Dear nappyhead:
Dear graying, dear balding, not lost, hard won: Dear wonder:
Dear sloping shoulders: Dear man-spread: Dear spread-legs:
Dear thick-thighs: Dear sandbag breasts, sandbag belly,
sandbag buttocks: Dear Bigfoot: Dear liquid hips:
Dear blistered nipples: Dear ears, dear fear, dear fingers,
dear fists:

       they're coming. stay ready.

Pleasure Insurrections I

There's an intersection in the River Oaks neck
of Houston, Texas where, I kid you not, *directly*

across the street from a Starbucks there's
another Starbucks and this, I assume, is to clearly

mark the gates of Hell for those who seek entry.
I consider it not at all coincidental that

these Starbuckses sit blocks from the most expensive
teardown in local memory. *Teardown*: when your pride is

too small to be seen from outer space. For real,
though, Hell's home to a boatload of scorned

creatives—folks whose use of color, of colorful
language never caught God's eye. *God*: another

tired metaphor for *gatekeeper*. While it's true that
any mammal can benefit from a well-timed

withdrawal, I find so many of y'all need to slap
a suffix on your *want*: let's get it *on,* people. Turn me

out, in other words. *On:* the piss-soaked direction
of moonlight. A southern exposure. *Out*: a gesture

toward. An expansion. A never-ending swelling.
A full-throated moan. Another becoming.

Pleasure Insurrections III

I know you'll call me a trickster—slick, as if
that's an icky thing to be—but I swear on each

of my stifled desires, in my immediate last life
I was a banana slug. Skin the color of spun sunshine,

ten inches long, where it counted; what
would you not give to be thus endowed? Yet

possessed of many genders, of lusts I am
yet afraid to name; when bent, sure, I could

get myself off, but I've always preferred the touch
of another. (I phrase it in the singular so you won't

think me a slithering thing: I know
what I am, I am.) In our pursuit of the fruit

we'd take the form of matter and myth—let time be
swallowed by the light, order by chaos, conviction

by doubt, entering each other
as if we were not impossible. We are. I typically don't

apologize for my proselytizing but forgive me this:
before we search for signs of life on other planets, before

we stipulate that there are white people in the future, how about
we situate ourselves in the now? I am hungry for this day.

Pleasure Insurrections IX

This is a poem about bees, but also, not. What I mean to say is that
this is a poem about bees, but it's not a nature poem. (Or it is. Of this
I am certain: it is nothing of nurture.) There's hundreds of tiny blush pink
flowers littering my front lawn—as if somebody's canny granny long ago
snatched fists-full of seeds from a burlap sack and pelted them

into the ever-changing winds, as tender, and the wind said I *commit you*
to the earth and let the seeds lay where they may, play where they wanted.
I never asked him to but my lawn guy seems to know to set the mower
to just the right height not to knock off their pretty little heads.
And wow, do those needy, greedy bees go to town. I half expect them

to drown, the way they dive in, reckless, spend the better part of the day
getting right drunk off these blooms, careening from
one cuplet to the next. (Their binge is proper work.) Still, most of them,
these bees, they quit around lunchtime, so yesterday, right about sundown,
when I stepped out my front door to greet the neighbor across the street

who either does or does not have a new boyfriend that's at least
twenty years older than he is I was stopped in my tracks by the sight
of a single bee, still, I presume, mad hungry, going at it *hard*, like
it was working extra shifts to earn cash to send home to its family
in Myanmar. Or maybe it's just that this bee is like me, a chub, a glutton,

a slut lustful for more of that gooey good stuff. My critics will print
what they must, call me a slag, while I and mine shall glisten our skin
with sea salt and time, and laugh, and laugh—

7 Ways to Say My Name

after Danez Smith

- faded blueprint for praising the graying of the day

- velvet-throated glimmer of need

- stiff kindling for the raging prayer

- gossamered shield, forged of the squall of myth

- locked strongbox, stilling the ruins of the hunt

- immortal verse, unearthed

- *Daddy*

Heliocentric Cento

after Sun Ra

I am

as you once were

an instrument
legend
skylight, blues, but
another kind of blue
rough house blues
blues *on planet mars*
velvet tapestry from an asteroid
the other side of the sun
the brother of the wind
the all of everything
the cosmic explorer
dreaming
the ninth eye
trying to find myself
after the end of the world

eternal retrospect
images (in a mirror)

the beginning of wounds

and something else—

the instrument
not a fantasy
not the kind that's blue:
big city blues,
blues, at midnight
a fireside chat with lucifer
soft talk, walking on the moon
the light thereof
the changing wind
the damned *air*
beyond the door of myth,
of mythic worlds
looking outward
outside the time zone
under different stars

dimensional reflections
of tomorrows never known

pleasure, immeasurable

Addendum

An abbreviated list of the universe
of shit I continue to fail to learn:
how to say *I'm sorry* and let
the words rust—hang there,
in the thinnest air, willed aloft
only by their indiscretion; the word
in any language for the moment
when you fall in love with someone
you've never ever met, face
to funny face; how to bare my belly
to the sun in full view of everyone
I say I love; how to say *I love you* while
pouring corn flakes into a chipped ceramic bowl
ringed with fading daisies, blue and yellow
and freed of bees and meaning; how
to look west, toward the sinking day, expose
my wetted cheek to anyone who wants
to wound me further; how not to feel
the bullets; how not to feel the bullets;
how to pronounce my name without
a knee on my neck; how not
to flee the bullets; how green can be
a minted thing that swaddles my toes
or saddles my back, depending on
the con; how to say *no more*; how
to say no more; how to point my
gun right at the right at the rite
at the riot and shoot; how to say *no,*
more; how to fly; how to fly, high;
how to rise above; how to heal;
how to heal; how to heel.

Think: The Voice of God

> *The voice of God, if you must know, is Aretha Franklin's.*
>   —attributed to Marianne Faithfull

I am far too huge to be reducible
by threat of proof. Think *power/house*.
Think *$50,000 wad of cash*. Think
Detroit, 1963. Think *she too big*

for Motown. Think gripping a mouse
of a *little prayer* and wrestling that ditty
up a mountain. Think stepping in for
your boy Luciano Pavarotti and putting

a little spank on some *Nessun Dorma*.
Think pushing past trouble's upper limits
and moving a president to tears. Think
standing *Oh*. Think [Freedom].

Lay some respect on My name. I am
The Queen: Father, Mother, and
wholy holy. A natural, I: ain't no way
no king ever gets one over on Me.

Midnight Mass, Prospect Park, Brooklyn

Once, I found salvation under the canopy
of an oak tree. Once, long past the half-light, I learned

> what it means to stand dead-center in the spiral,
> to subscribe to an astronomical model

in which I am the Sun. Once the moon, seduced,
lost all sense of proportion and, lusty, spread

> the leaves of that sheltering oak to limn me
> in silverleaf, as if to myth me—to render me

liquid, shape-shifting; to reflect the wonder
of me back unto me—was the point of its being. Once

> their offspring—the sons of the oak and the moon
> and the night—were called to my glistening, stiffened

by the thick of me. There, then, limbs slick with want,
we cupped the sublime in ourselves and each other.

Acknowledgments

Thanks to the editors of the journals in which the following poems in *Bound* originally appeared:

Across the Margin: "Mule"
Honey Literary: "Pleasure Insurrections III," "Questionnaire I"
Kweli Journal: "Heliocentric Cento"
Phi Beta Kappa Forum: "Breath"
Southern Humanities Review: "Addendum"

"N'Jadaka's Appeal" was originally published in Foglifter Press' *Home is Where You Queer Your Heart* anthology.

"7 Ways to Say My Name" was originally published in *VINCENT*, Millay Arts' Journal of Art-in-Residence.

All words in "Heliocentric Cento" (except for the word "Cento") come from Sun Ra album and song titles and lyrics/verses.

In the poem "Queer Fan Fiction: Frida & Josephine @ La Casa Azul," the italicized verses *wanting you is my offence / you have all the evidence / now I wait for you to sentence me* are lyrics from the song "My Fate Is in Your Hands," recorded by Josephine Baker in 1929.

Following is the poem "Goddam Cento" with endnotes indicating by whom the poems' phrases were originally written. (The "Goddam" in the title is inspired by Nina Simone's "Mississippi Goddam.")

> And when I descended to the valleys and the plains
> God was there also, [1] *God*, again, all *up* in the Kool-Aid. [2]
> Antic God, [3] aphrodisiac God, [4] without one friend, [5]

another gorgeous thing that should not have happened. (6)
(My God, why did I turn my eyes upward (7) as if He were
weightless? (8) A little flying God Almighty in the sky, (9)

the beating of the wings, unheard.) (10) All day I keep hearing
the fighting in the valley. (11) Dear God for whom I am
one green marble: (12) why do you hide behind your mask

(the sun and stars)? (13) Show yourself. (14) You lied to me,
all these years. (15) I do not mean to be fatalistic: (16)
if to be a God means to consider (17) the fact of my own

demise, (18) what I once was and where I have been—(19) a body
that turns toward openness, fantasy—(20) then I am God,
we are God, (21) whose beloved breath becomes (at last) our own (22)

1 "God," Khalil Gibran
2 "God Letter, " CM Burroughs
3 "oh antic God", Lucille Clifton
4 "[A black God touched me today . . .] ," Jon Leon
5 "God," Langston Hughes
6 "Oh God," Michelle Tea
7 "God, God," Fleda Brown
8 "My God, It's Full of Stars," Tracy K. Smith
9 "Their God," Harriet Monroe
10 "Wings of a God," Denise Levertov
11 "The Gods," W. S. Merwin
12 "Dear God," Susan Abraham
13 "God-Lover," Muriel Safford
14 "Dear Big Gods," Mona Arshi
15 "Mississippi Goddam," Nina Simone
16 "About God & Things," Wanda Coleman
17 "Not a God," Carl Dennis
18 "God!" Phillip Miller
19 "God Particles," James Crews
20 God on the Treadmill," Benjamin S. Grossberg
21 Jubi Arriola-Headley
22 "Kissing God Goodbye," June Jordan

With Unmitigated Gratitude...

To the poet Lillian-Yvonne Bertam, who helped me realize what *Bound* could be, and has become.

To Gabriel Fried and the good folk at Persea Books, who've given *Bound* a home.

To the poets Victoria Chang, Gabrielle Calvocoressi, and John Keene, whose generous words about this collection melted my heart and my brain, and whose own transcendent contributions to the craft and community of poetry light the path for me.

To the good folk at Yaddo, Millay Arts, and the Virginia Center for the Creative Arts, who provided me with space and time and support to write many of the poems in this collection.

To John Foster, graphics guy extraordinaire, who helped me achieve the final form of "Heliocentric Cento."

To all the folks I thanked in *Original Kink,* and so many poets, writers, and others I've met since—you are still and will ever be part of my journey, my community.

To my mother, who I, shit of a son that I am, *failed* to thank in *Original Kink*—because, if I'm being honest, I wasn't sure she'd want to be associated with my brand of kink. Silly me—I love you, Mummy, and I'm going to work hard to get more comfortable discussing my poems with you. On that note: read "Caribbean Gothic | Four Women" first. Lotta you in that one. Maybe "Requiem" next—short poem, but much to discuss. (Read "Questionnaire I" at your own risk.)

To Paulo, for so much, not the least of which how he helps my mother, when we're visiting her and I've long gone to bed and they stay up late, drinking cognac and talking deep, explains me to her, and helps her manage her expectations of me.

To all my ancestors, both known and unknown, who I carry with me and who I suspect regularly gift me verse, often in the most surprising of ways.

To all y'all—if you're holding this collection in your hands, thank you. Go on, flip to any page—let's play.